Lake Effect

Poems

by Sara Quinn Rivara

ISBN-13: 978-0615819952

Aldrich Press
24600 Mountain Ave, Unit 35
Hemet, California 92544

Acknowledgements

"Tree of Heaven" first appeared in *32 Poems Magazine*

"Love Charm" and "Bible Study" first appeared in *The Cortland Review*

"Family Vacation, Last Date With Narcissus" and "In The Fields of Asphodel, Evening" in *Blackbird*

"A White Dress is Toxic, Much Like Acid Rain" in *Bluestem*

"Persephone Marooned in the Underworld" in *Literary Mama*

"South Haven" and "Mackinac Island" in *Cream City Review*

Table of Contents

A White Dress is Toxic, Much like Acid Rain

...you did not choose to be in the story of the woman
in the white dress which was as cool and
evil as a glass of radioactive milk.
—"Like, God," Lynn Emanuel

Except that I did. I stood beneath the chokecherry
tree stunned by the welter and muck of June

(bugs trilling in the bog, insects thick-bodied
as fingers, fists, the sweet weight of a baby's
wrist—), I professed loveandfidelity and till-death

do-we-pluck-out-our-eyes. And before someone could sling
a shotgun and shanghai me out of that wet dream, I was the cream

in *his* coffee, before grace and bereavement milk-poured
themselves like honeysuckle (a child suckled

at my breast three years later and I knew
out of this life is the only living left) vines across my throat:

I clutched that clot of the cosmos, love, faced the forced
march of the hamstrung heart
into a swarm of angry bees—

Love Charm

On the table an empty bowl. The garden a funeral
of moths. Cup plant brimming with last night's
rain. Dawn. Lawn laced with frost. A few scraps

of dinner balance on the compost heap: melon.
Lettuce. At the hinge-creak, bright eyed things
scuttle back toward the shadowy edge of the yard

near the pond, the dark heart of everything.
The back porch damp. I close the garden
gate. The trail is narrow—gravel, then dirt, then deer-

track.I put my feet in the slender hoof-hollows
of a young doe, and keep walking. The way thick
with burdock, wild chervil. The air full of bull

frog and warbler. Geese southbound. The dogs clamber on
ahead, noses to the ground, dew spangling the soft
underfur of their bellies. Here, the pond opens her mouth

to the stream; a log blistered with frogs; pale mounds
of sweetbread mushrooms bloom. The last trees
in the orchard curve over the trail, sway quietly

in small wind. This is where I buried the charm: a knife, pearl-
handled and flecked with rust, beneath the apple trees. A battered
blade. A sparrow's heart. A weapon to slit love's slender

throat. The dogs circle back, begin to head for home. The orchard
struck with fireblight, only a few bitter windfalls on the ground. So.
The wind's picked up just right: a few leaves scuttle past,

a hatch of flies swarm over the pond. Love shakes his little rattle
in the eastern sky: how slowly I walk toward the house! The
   windows
are blank, a trail of smoke from the chimney and a light flicks on

in the kitchen where my husband waits,
his lips just shaping my name.

Family Vacation

Have you ever thought that you're crazy?
They have been driving for four hours. The Mackinac
Bridge looms ahead of them. She is terrified

of bridges, open water, falling. She cannot
swim. She will not ask him to drive.
Have you ever thought that you need help? This

is the most he's said on the subject
of love. *I'm just joking. You've lost
your sense of humor. Christ.*

His hand reaches for her knee. He pushes
up the thin cotton of her sun
dress, fingers the elastic of her underwear.

*If I drive you could go down
on me. It'd be fun. Why don't you
take a chance? The baby will sleep. He'll*

*never know. Have a little adventure
once in a while. Why do you have
to be so frigid?*

The bridge is built to sway. This is what keeps
it from snapping.

Stop it, she says. *Stop.* He does. For
a while.

Once she asked him if he had
an inner life. *What do you mean?
Like guts? Like my intestines?*

The bridge is five miles
long. The Straits below are dangerous and the bridge
was a triumph. This is what she learned

from the travel brochure. In St. Ignace, they stop
at a reststop that sells Indian drums, rolling papers,
Petosky stones. She buys a drum for the baby.

He gums it, beats it against the car seat, chews
the wooden handle. She lets
the man drive. Beneath the car

the water seems to be made of rough stone
and she tries to focus on the car in front
of her. Sea birds swoop down

from the bearings to the water below.
Soon, his hand cups the back of her head,
thumb stroking her ear. *Relax,* he says.

We're not going to fall in. He pushes
her head down, already un-
zipping his jeans. She does nothing

to stop him. She imagines water.
Waves. The great stones at the bottom
of the Straits.

Tree of Heaven

*The ailanthus tree, also known as the tree-of-heaven, is an exotic, invasive
species whose flowers have an offensive odor.*

The world has broken blazing: snow spun
sugar in the tamarack swamp, the dogs panting

from their walk, our garden spent
and cluttered with winter's waste:

the slow winnowing away of the spirit,
barren winter field of the heart. Today, walking the dogs
my few moments of contentment: Atwater wellhead ice-bound,

cattail reeds glazed with sun. Face flush with walking
my husband pointed at two giant swans
standing on the frozen fen behind the dry gold

of old reeds. They watched back, suspicious. A small wind
wove its way through his hair, mine. But he was impatient
to complete the task: a walk. We retraced our steps

down the long trail, heads down in the wind. Then back home,
ailanthus tapping its thin branches on the window, its thousand
seedlings covered in graying snow. Television

clicked back on, blinds shut, the world and all its space
denied.
       I put my heart back in its gilded box. Outside,
fields of winter rye shaking in cold wind,

wild swans and their whole lives in the fen.
Only a few months before spring, until
something inside of me will break or be broken for good:

headwaters edged with ice, swans,
fields brilliant as blades—
and the stinking tree of heaven springing up unwanted, everywhere.

Bible Study

Behind the Red Lobster, the sky leveled off into lake: static
from the radio. Late model Pontiac. Body glitter. Hades' hot
hand on my thigh. *Why not, Lenten Rose?* he cried. How high
Orion leaped above the waves! Something burned, something
trembled between us: was me at once, singing. No, was
the cotton shirt tearing. No, was the tampon flung
in the sand. No. Was his hand. *You blood-star, you
earthworm heart!* It tore me apart. Except for stars, I was
lost. A swallow sipped my cup of trembling and the Pleiades
hung their shirts on his nail. Hell, I licked willingly; I kicked
out the windows and yelled. Scaffolded my skin against
his tree. I, small girl, got laid. Him—my salvaged wreck, my salted
    blade—

Last Date With Narcissus

See how the water reflects the shore?
he said. Instead, it absorbed; dull
as the wounds of the dead. We watched
plovers guard their nests, a lip of light whipstitch
the horizon. Night seeped up like a gas

and anesthetized, love-dumb, I, demure girl
echoed as he talked about himself. The Lake
grappled with the sky; how he flattered! One log
left of the old dock. He whispered, cajoled,
pulled out his cock. Sand like salt, a pillar

of tree. I shrugged, said *why not?* There was a curl
of wind, a scatter of seeds. I suffered a kind
of blindness: I loved him back. *It's not
that you're unattractive,* he said. South Manitou
Island lowered its ursine head. The lake steeled

itself beneath the sky. Beachgrass, jackpine, sand.
A field of narcissus by the two-track road. The bay
beckoned *memory, forget*. He held my hand, clutched
the back of my head. *It's not that I don't love
you,* his back in the swale. The dead in the deep
sang of shipwreck and gale. I realized his heart
was a mirror, a silvered glass: flawed, it showed only

his face back. And that imperfect icon saw me
not at all—not lake, not sky, not human breath. A flower
with a yellow center. Then I put his hand down.
I swallowed my heart: I let that man drown.

Drought 1

Catch crows on the tip of your tongue, swallow. Eat the small eggs
of a wren, lick your milky palm. A quart of foxes in the berry

bucket. Eat bullets, eat blackberries, marginalia creamed with
    spinach
leaves, garlic, cowbane, hogweed: eat this, you'll die; touch this,
    you'll

go blind. North of Cadillac, fields of wind machines fan the flames.
Mount Pleasant a shriveled fruit. Kalamazoo brown as a goat. Leak
    milk

into the wooden bowl, unsheath the bulbs from their sockets,
    flower
from its pistol, undo those creamy blossoms. Eat your hat, eat your
    words,

crow perched on the tip of your tongue, word that won't come.
    Mackinac
floats its turtled back into the Straits. My son cartwheels: incline,
    rock,

juniper: he's fine. I'm floundering. Tuck your hand into mine, child;
Lake Huron mops the sky with its blue hair. The bicycles tremble.
    Rabbits,

mergansers. It isn't fair, any of it. The horizon drapes itself across
    the bridge, all blue
trembling, all vine unstoppered. All of that space, open. Such
    burning as this—

Persephone, Marooned in the Underworld

In the grayest month of the year, lake-fog
curdled between whitepine stands, grouse burrowed
in lacy snow-caves, I let the bird from
its cage, unshackled the houseplants, undressed

the Christmas tree. The radio crackled
into dry air: carols, disaster. The snow fell
faster. Against the window the parakeet
thumped, lay stunned on the sill; still,

I kept cleaning. Clouds gouged the western
sky as a cold front pushed over the lake: graupel
and electricity. Snow fine as ash. The little heart
kept beating, panicked. Then my son woke

from his nap, plucked the bird from the sill, tucked
it beneath his arm. Gently put it back in the cage, *it's*

all right, it's all right, he was singing. The sky
broke apart above the white field.

Lake House

The lake's raw lace-edge; cuttooth moon, loons
knife beneath foam: spring, unsheathing. A couple kissed

on the dock, some dumb fool strummed a guitar. A few
men on the pier cast their lines for salmon, hope

roped their heads like thorns. Oh, what's to notice? Fool
girl, love-numb, salt, alone, dumbstruck, her sweater bunched

beneath her arms, two damp moons bloomed. Beach houses
     mooned
over the street; all empty-dark, a few dishes in the sink, mildew

a knife, a pear, a winding sheet. Taste of blood, few fool
stars behind the clouds' trembling shroud. A man and a woman

rolled over and over each other in the sand. Someone
humming. And hope slaked out in rivulets. Unspooled.

Sara, unweep yourself. Birds fill the sky's blue till.
All the world scraped off or swept up. All singing scattered, stilled.

In the Fields of Asphodel, Evening

falls head over heels down the shallow embankment, spills
costume jewelry from its pockets—gold lockets, glass beads,
    diamond
rings, enameled bees. Dead carp rise from the field and swarm

around your knees: mouths agape, the hook set and yanked—
Persephone tripped down this ravine where night unspools
from thrushthroat; twine and fishline. It waylays you on the picnic

table before the cops arrive. It's never on time. Is the root
of the tree, the field forgetting its level; it caterwauls, pries
off the lid. Drums daylight into dirt, earthworms the eyes

of the dead. Sighs to the sycamores; is witches' broom, fireblight.
Doesn't care if you, naked and curled in the crook of its arm,
are alright. Is the last words you loved: *wilderness. Incandescent.*

The brine of sex. The taste after. Turns off every light in the house;
tongues the toaster, outpours the Big Dipper. Tells you after all
you're not the girl it loves; grows stiffer, limper. Ventriloquists

frog over the swamp mallow, divorces the past. It *isn't* you it loves
but the turned curve of hillock, rootknot. A field of narcissus
in the rain. Feels like a ballpeen hammer; sounds like keening,
    sounds

like clamor. Cleaves the whiteoak, cleaves onto the body and
    forgets
you were even there. *Were* you there? Your body is a field-ravaged
ruin. It befuddles the thrush, baffles the moon. Is a sugar-tit

of reassurance (repeat *I'm fine, I'm fine, I'm fine).* Milk light. Meal
worms. Maggots. Floats the ferry across the straights, is the
    grinning
abyss—it lies. It whines: paperwhites and a dark steed. Chokes

on your mouthful of seeds. It undermines. Lizard, bone, dust
    halfway
between heaven and hell sounds a bell. Charon's boat
eases through waist-high reeds. Tell him you've mouthed your
    coins,

lift up the meat of your tongue. Every soft place leads to this—it's
    either Lethe
or bliss. Hand over your sorrows, cross the tangled line. This is the
    last
blessing. Look: your body has begun to shine.

The House Was Full of Bees

in the eaves, dripping from the bathroom faucet, furred knives
in bedsheets. In the kitchen cabinets, the salts, and the gallon

of expired milk, the box of Borax, the toothpaste, the silk
chemise; in my hair, my mouth, the pupil's dark ponds

where swans drift like empty boats: seething, humming, singing,
honey dripping from the walls, from your tongue, from

the laundry strung on the wire between the house and the dead
elm. The bees clot, knot and undo, knot and undo the seam

the selvage, affix themselves like buttons to my chest—
hush, hush, love, doves are in the cupboard, mice have made nests

of your hair and the queen is lost and the hive is wild
with terror. Allelu the grasses, the praying masses

all honey and hickory and meat flayed tender and sweet!
Praise be the empty chair, the child curled in bed, the mother's

guilt, the curdled milk; adulate in the garden, swords hilt-
deep in mud. Who drags herself from the cold bed, the empty

dawn, the body untouched for years? Praise be enmity, solstice,
ash, the jagged pier into the froth; praise be the drought, the
    unloved,

the wife who leaves; praise be the unswept floor, moldy bread, the
    clogged
drain. O! Praise be the peony, the stain—

South Haven

Remember how the Pleiades hung stunned over the culvert, their
   breasts
swaying over Orion's open maw, his hands raw? I didn't blink.
   Lake Michigan

gnawed the shore: granite, plinth, all that was left of it—the old life.
Memory, that mouth full of ash, highway that only runs south

where the power plant pumps into the sluice. Fish swim backward,
the land tilts, headland, snowbank, bluff. The pier draped in silver
   cloths

all night, lighthouse erect and comely as a lover, that red
knife; ten years a housewife and mute. Struck numb since

I stripped down: wool sweater, lace, wire. Grace. Yes, this
old thing again—unpeel the nametag, that name is lost

tossed in the ravine where narcissus grows out of season,
girls kiss each other between the knees. *Hello my name is*

fades to *Hell is.* This place: headland, pier, glacial drift. Beer
cans glint like satellites and Hades clomps around the basement

like an oaf. Home where beach scours the sky, the milk sours,
hope ruffles its feathers. Oh, who unseals the sky's blue dome?
   Who

calls this blear world home but the rest of us? The rest. Sara: the
   Pleiades
pour down their terrible fire: all winter, the flowers bloomed.

Mackinac Island

Penelope, Undone

Undo the cotton shift, those sprigs of wild horsemint,
those buttons of ripe butter! Beauty,
you're weeping. Then the girlskin unhinged, fur

and skin, all silver scar and painted lip, pointed nail enameled
as: undo the sky, lion-heart. Untell each lie, untie the moorings
and sail beyond the still harbor. Oh, best beast: unsheath those
   bleached

teeth. The bloodied lip bleats best, and so the whole
bloody heap is in a pile in the sand: all that hide, all that
fancy. And the jays are on it and the crows

pick apart even the bones. Even the lacework of veins
and the meaty heart. To walk away (headland, long grass, clear
water) is another thing completely. To not look back on the old

life is salt, lozenge. All carved off ears, while up here
the air clears out that thought alley. Who told these suitors
to make a line at the gate? To bring bread and honey, milkweed

nosegays and their hard meat? The verdant flesh
is failing. This, thigh. This sow's ear, this lemonrind. This
limestone cliff, this turtled island? All mine, all mine.

To the Suitor, Unwanted (yet) Desired

Come, undresser of lakesand, of tampon, of field sparrow,
merganser, loon. Uvular, dust. Insert here your coins,
crank *this,* rattle. I unhand it: calyx, ruby-throated hummer.
Well, I'm taken, old sport. You're the single gal's last

resort? Not what I seek. Rather, a field of bees. Locust
trees. Salty undercarriage of—. Undulate, too late.
Compost shot through with seeds, invasive and spectacular.
Gold-rimmed. Asphalt melts beneath these girlpelts. Acidic

as a bog, it stalls the cogs of *your* great machine. This girl burns,
learns French, learns *l'histoire des femmes.* Which is to say, the
    history
of a dog. Shorebirds poach dead fish from sodden logs. Do I bore
    you
too? The line of men snakes out the door, some in the hedge, some

in the pantry, the great empty bed. Take a number. Upend the trees.
The grasses undo from the sky's blue loom. The moon empties
its pretty face into the Lake. It pools around my feet.

Yes and Yes

—for Jonah

Wild roses explode beside the narrow road; limestone cliffs ease
away: acid and water wash down like hope over the turtle's holy
     back,
the wild gasp of the world. Mergansers dive and dive and dive
     again

and wind whittles the escarpment; the arch winnows. For this
I put out the light, left home, abandoned the dogs, came
here where it smells of balsam, horses, false elderberry. Where
     muskrat

once dove far beneath the waves, where ships were wrecked,
where the earth was new and dark. And you, little bird, wholly
yourself beside me as the sun sets over the Straits and Mackinac

pedals into night: you, separate universe I pushed into the world,
     half
my fucked DNA, half my heart cleaved clean away: may you row
     out, know
joy, unmoor yourself; may you bloom and bloom into lake-combed
     sand
into the meat and storm of this burgeoning *and—*

Fish of Michigan

It happened despite, it happened *nevermind*
the innerlife. It happened while the breeze unraveled
the rug on its loom, the shuttle slowed, the door swung

in the sweet breeze. All this time, and *that's* what I meant:
stinkpot turtle, muskrat, muskellunge, balsam, alder, ash—
Such are the names of freedom, honey: full bodied. Hungry.

The sky pounds its blue drum and frogs spawn, tadpoles burn
their evolutionary fires: legs like the first bud of the hybrid lilac,
jack-in-the-pulpit's slim Edwardian throat: drink *me*. This flesh

burns. This trick turned ugly beneath the arborvitae on *that*
suburban cul-de-sac, the creek all feral-catandvole. Weed
and teenagers fucking in the flickering light of the wellhouse,

the engines hum-drumming all night. All the houses
flush with water pressure. Well, that's dead. That's five miles
beneath the Mackinac Bridge. Fish in the cold waters

of the Straits. O Michigan, Michigan! The world hangs
on a hinge. There's so much living to do in my own skin.

Drought 2

My son drapes hope's bright horizon over his shoulders as easily
as I'd throw a sweater, my hair, the scraps of a sandwich into the
   dry

air. But what of that other horizon, bound circle, loneliness
of a day in the swamp woods, buttonbush and tamarack,
   blacksnake,

grackle, crow-shadow of anxiety cicada-thumping in the dead
elm? My son runs on ahead of me, his knees dirt-rubbed, deliberate

in their futurity. Birds of all kinds knock their hollow wings
against the sky. Here, I fit the boundary against my heart: if I touch

you, I'll flake off. I'll dust-and-treble. Body-thralled, female,
   wanting—
Desire's dull blade flat against my little woman's thumb. Lake
   Michigan

binds the beach to its side, marsh rose humps on by as I follow
that wisp into the wood. Yesterday's hope a spent gun, just a touch

and I'm done, fallen apart and terrorized. An arm: *there*. The press
   of your breath on the small cup of my throat and--unwind. Fen

moss; I'm unzipped. I'm field, spent. Pearly everlasting sun
   shocked
onto death. Oh, not a stick, but a heart that can break and break.

Sign

Jesus said to the woman, "your faith has saved you. Go in peace." Luke 7:50

What saves but faith in things, the dry well, the irritant, the
    handmaid,
piano, bauble, bayonet. The house wren's nest left
on the compost heap, the rake, the lock, the closed door—and I
    still

want more? Vicissitudes. If you. And then. Bender, prayer. Lake's
    temper
and taste, collar to my thirst, colder around my bare waist. One day
she's in her blue robe, the next she's murdered the children,
    drowned

everyone but the rats. The fat sun heaves over the empty
trees and the woman I was went home, brushed her hair. The
    woman
I've become clambers from the boat, no jar to be filled. This is not

a love poem. This is not a charm, a pipe, a bird. It lifts its song
above the waves and from the crow's lonely throat a plume of
    moths
contrails the sky above the dirt. This is not suburban, not an
    exercise,

not valve or attention. Not sex, not breath. This is not Miami
    Avenue,
or Boylan Street, abandoned mill, not the landfill, sluggish river,
not loneliness.
Not regret. A sky filled with birds. A sky filled with air.

This is not scared. Not the woman who held her breath for thirteen
years. Not blear. This is the future. This is the open palm.
Is psalm. Trees cradle the sky. Is this the point of liftoff?

The garden grows wilder every afternoon. Soon, crows gather
and pick at the hem of my yellow dress, weasels wear
their wedding rings like amulets. And in the woods a bear stirs

in her luxurious furs—that old song? It's done. Let me say it
again: autumn came and opened its borders, split open my chest.
All the words climbed out.

Fata Morgana

Crow in the dead elm. God's heart: dianthus and blight. Inbetween
the Lake balances her cold scales.

(Was)

What kind of woman are you anyway? Burned the wedding dress.
Sky above me pressed its knees together. Palisades' nuclear

glow warm as a man's tongue on my thigh. Fireflies and lies and
Michigan's furred mitt across my eyes: in this story, I point the gun

at his heart and pull the trigger. Stella Maris, oh Mother of
    Sleeping
Bear, mother of drowned children, failed swimmers, the faint
    glimmer

that lips the horizon. Prayerful, I lie down, naked and trembling.
    I'm just
*that kind of woman. Hysteric. Mock-orange overgrows the garden
    gate, apples*

testicular in the orchard. Weeds. Chicago's hard lights hammer the
    West.
The Lake unclothes the wanton shore. *Je suis la dame qui. Sans
    merci. Plus*

belle. Home is where the heart is scraping the scales from its eyes.
    You
are not the woman you thought you were. But you're this

one. But you're instead: Our Lady of the Lake and the world's a
    made
thing: child curled and sleeping on my chest, word uncleaving,
    incarnate,

shamble. Birds skirt the valves, the foamy edge, the mirage
shimmers over the water: those silver towers, that cloven heart.

Solstice

This isn't the poem that composts, that will bring
you a cup of tea in the leaky evening light. This isn't

the poem that clouds up the windows on your father's Chevy;
it won't lick the sweat from your nape, won't break

what already broke: teacup, self, cheap elastic
around your thigh, sky ferris-wheeled toward the Lake.

Weeds disciple the field: O Mother of Tongues! Eastern cottontails
nest in the grass like abandoned children. This poem

sails its little boat into the harbor without any lights, knows
love is blind, has eyes like black cherries, two heads sewn

on the neck of the yearling lamb. Empty your purse of elegies:
    gloss
pink as an Easter ham, that naked little man strung up in a tree

and the altar studded with bees. This poem will knot burrs
in your hair. It knows: need, keening, ash. It doesn't care;

it litters. It glitters; it wants, always, more. This poem smells
like the Lake in summer, it leans against the reeds, it bleeds

in its new white dress and it will hold your shoulder with such
tenderness. O Poem! Will you love me after the rumpled bed

and the harp? This is the poem that cries out *you knew
it would come to this, sweetheart.* Your heart strung up

like meat and the butcher sharpens his knives. Your son's hand pressed against your face, your own soft body, your

distress, your beautiful mess. The poem has overcome itself with blood, with blossom—

Instructional Design

In this new life is there a man who calls me lovely
and do I care? Little blue flame, gundamp twilight, lift
me into evening's last air: cadenza me against the credenza,
carve the rules upon my hair. Cicadas whine. I've left the place

where nothing was fine, that backwards glance, old rag
on my brow. That was the past and I've choked it. So press
your muzzle against my neck, set all the atomic clocks back.
Lay the ladder against the eaves, cleave onto me. Bible-thump

me awake. It's *me* I want to save, leap headlong into Lake,
headlands grass-woven, wind-harped. The scarp sharp
and unkempt, beach rose, the unstopped mouth: what I'm saying
is a woman can only flay herself once. Sinew, scrap: I've
    taxidermied

all that. Made this honed thing, this blessing. This life. What I hold
in my hands I own: the bones of a dead crow, the augur, the ashes
of some dead girl who rolled away the stone: Baby, climb up
these branches of unsoured sky, the puddle of my eye, hold me

against reason; all guns are permitted this season, and I'm alone
in these woods. I've gathered all the flowers, all the bullets I could.

About the Author

Sara Quinn Rivara was born and raised in the suburbs of Chicago, and has lived most of her life on the shores of Lake Michigan. She received her MFA in poetry from the Warren Wilson College Program for Writers. She single parents, works as a semi-professional classical singer, teaches English and Writing at Kalamazoo Valley Community College, and lives in Kalamazoo, Michigan with her son Jonah.

Made in the USA
San Bernardino, CA
24 September 2013